Requirements Elicitation Interviews and Workshops
Simply Put!

Best Practices, Skills, and Attitudes for Requirements Gathering on IT Projects

Thomas Hathaway
Angela Hathaway

Copyright © 2016 BA-EXPERTS

All rights reserved. No part of this publication may be reproduced, distributed, or transmitted in any form or by any means, including photocopying, recording, or other electronic or mechanical methods, without the prior written permission of the publisher, except in the case of brief quotations embodied in critical reviews and certain other noncommercial uses permitted by copyright law.

Ordering Information:

Quantity sales. Special discounts are available on quantity purchases by corporations, associations, and others. For details, contact the publisher at books@BusinessAnalysisExperts.com.

The content of this book is also available as an eCourse at http://businessanalysisexperts.com/product/video-course-elicitation-interviews-workshops/

ISBN-10: 1522965831
ISBN-13: 978-1522965831

DEDICATION

This work is dedicated to future generations of Business Analysts, Product Owners, Subject Matter Experts, Domain Experts, COOs, CEOs, Line Managers, and anyone responsible for representing the business community's interests on an Information Technology project.

CONTENTS

DEDICATION i

CONTENTS ii

ACKNOWLEDGMENTS iv

PREFACE v

Introduction to Requirements Interviews and Workshops 7
    What Exactly Is "Requirements Elicitation" and Who Needs It Anyway? 7

Best Practices for Requirements Interviews 12
    Proper Preparation Prevents Poor Performance 12
    Starting a Requirements Interview on the Right Foot 15
    Performing under Pressure 18
    Make Sure You Can Talk the Talk 22
    Maintain Control throughout the Requirements Interview 24
    Closing the Requirements Interview in Style 27

Characteristics of an Effective Requirements Interviewer 32
    Personable People Have a Head Start 32
    Maintaining Momentum during the Requirements Interview 35
    Using Active and Informational Listening to Hear Requirements 37
    Impediments to Effective Listening 40
    Overcoming the Impediments 43

Helping Stakeholders Discover Requirements 47

What Are the Five Elicitation Approaches and Which Is the Simplest for Starters 47

Informal Requirements Interviews 49

Formal, Face-to-Face Requirements Interviews 51

Requirements Elicitation Using Email 55

Teleconferencing for Requirements 57

Requirements Gathering Workshops 60

How to Run a Requirements Gathering Workshop 64

How Requirements Gathering Workshops Work 64

Planning and Preparing for a Productive Requirements Gathering Workshop 67

How to Perform During the Workshop 71

Polishing and Publishing the Workshop Results 74

The Business Case for Requirements Workshops 76

Requirements Interviews and Workshops Wrap-Up 79

What Do You Do Next? 79

ABOUT THE AUTHORS 82

ACKNOWLEDGMENTS

This publication would not have been possible without the active support and hard work of our daughter, Penelope Hathaway. We would also be remiss if we did not acknowledge the thousands of students with whom we have had the honor of working over the years. We can honestly say that every single one of you influenced us in no small way.

Finally, we would like to acknowledge Harvey, the fictional Pooka created by Mary Chase and made famous by the movie of the same name with James Stewart. Very early in our marriage we recognized that a third entity is created and lives whenever we work closely on a concept, a new idea, or a new product. Over the years, this entity became so powerful and important to us that we decided to name it Harvey and he should rightfully be listed as the author of this and all of our creative works. Unfortunately, Harvey remains an invisible being, living somewhere beyond our physical senses but real nonetheless. Without Harvey, neither this book nor any of our other publications would have been possible. For us, Harvey embodies the entity that any collaborative effort creates and he is at least as real as each of us. We would truly be lost without him.

PREFACE

What is "Requirements Elicitation" and why should you care? Why should anyone read a book about gathering requirements? All you have to do to get the requirements for anything is ask everyone involved what they want, right? If you are capable of understanding their answers, you should be done in a heartbeat. So, why the fuss?

Based on the track record of the Information Technology (IT) profession, it appears that gathering the right requirements from the right people to define the right IT solution for any organization is nearly impossible. Industry insiders cannot even agree on what to call the process. Over the years, we have tried "Requirements Gathering", "Requirements Capture", "Requirements Definition", "Requirements Discovery", and "Requirements Elicitation". Regardless what we call it, this book will give you a head start on getting the job done right.

"Requirements Elicitation Interviews & Workshops Simply Put! - Best Practices, Skills, and Attitudes for Requirements Gathering on IT Projects" deals with the soft skills side of life, meaning skills, attitudes and behaviors that promote effective requirements elicitation. In particular, you can learn how to:

- ☑ Define and distinguish five specific requirements elicitation approaches from one-on-one Requirements Interviews to Requirements Gathering Workshops

- ☑ Evaluate the pros and cons of each approach for your organization and your project

- ☑ Use informational and active listening to capture hidden requirements

- ☑ Prepare, perform, and manage effective Requirements Gathering Workshops

- ☑ Recognize the challenges and strengths of facilitated Requirements Workshops with cross-functional groups of stakeholders

☑ Improve your interviewing skills by analyzing the best-practice attitudes and characteristics of effective interviewers

You can learn more business analysis techniques by visiting the Business Analysis Learning Store at

(http://businessanalysisexperts.com/business-analysis-training-store/)

to see a wide selection of business analysis books, eCourses, virtual and face-to-face instructor-led training, as well as a selection of FREE Business Analysis training.

Meanwhile, please enjoy this eBook. We appreciate any comments, suggestions, recommended improvements, or complaints that you care to share with us. You can reach us via email at eBooks@businessanalysisexperts.com.

INTRODUCTION TO REQUIREMENTS INTERVIEWS AND WORKSHOPS

This chapter will help you:

- Decide whether this book is right for you based on the course goals and objectives

- Judge where Requirements Elicitation fits in Agile or Waterfall methodologies

What Exactly Is "Requirements Elicitation" and Who Needs It Anyway?

Requirements define the future. If you do not define your future, you have no expectations and must be willing to accept whatever comes your way. In the world of Information Technology (IT), requirements define exactly what future applications will do and how they will meet the business needs when they go into production.

Unfortunately, every analysis of IT project performance over the past 70 some odd years pinpointed missing and misunderstood requirements as the major cause of project overruns and failures. This is such a well-known problem in the software industry that we created a profession called "Business Analysis" to address it.

The original idea was to let someone who could understand the business domain extract what the business community needed and wanted the software to do. That person should then express those needs and wants in the form of software requirements that IT professionals could understand and implement.

Very early on, those tasked with requirements elicitation had an epiphany. They discovered that it is impossible to define software requirements *in isolation*. Since changes to the software affect how the organization would work in the future, the requirements have to include how people would interact with the application. Changing people's behavior also requires changes in personnel training. Furthermore, software changes influence workflow causing procedural updates and automating tasks lead to changes in managerial responsibilities. Modifying existing or implementing new IT applications inevitably initiate a cascade of change that can be difficult to predict

Simply put, those responsible for gathering requirements for the software have to elicit the requirements for the entire *business solution* of which the software is just one component, albeit an integral one.

In today's world, we recognize business analysis as the process of eliciting (aka gathering, discovering, capturing, defining, etc.) and managing the requirements that any business solution has to meet. The question now has become, **"Who should be responsible for defining the future of the business?"**

Many organizations created full-time positions responsible for that challenging task. The people responsible for requirements elicitation typically have the job title "Business Analyst", "Business Systems Analyst", "Application Architect", or something similar. However, many people in organizations of any size gather requirements although they are not aware of it nor do they have any of those job titles.

To emphasize our support for both groups who bear this awesome responsibility, we avoid using job titles like "Business Analyst". We refer instead to 'the one wearing the BA hat'. Regardless of job title, whenever you are responsible for expressing business needs in requirements that solution providers (e.g., developers, testers, designers, trainers, etc.) have to understand, you are the one wearing the BA hat.

Of course, even as the one wearing the BA hat, you presumably do not have the authority to define the future of the business on your own. You need input from other people potentially affected by the future business solution to ensure that it will meet their business needs. In a word, you need **their requirements**.

How can you identify everyone in the organization that the proposed application could affect? Once you have identified them, how can you get each to contemplate and communicate their future business needs without knowing what the proposed IT solution would do? In other words, "How can you perform the slippery process of requirements elicitation when you are the one wearing the BA hat? What techniques can you use? How can you even get started?". Unfortunately for the one wearing the BA hat, getting other stakeholders to express their needs and wants vis-à-vis a proposed IT solution is a non-trivial challenge.

To meet that challenge, we propose that you need to hone your interpersonal skills, in particular your interviewing skills. If you have never interviewed another person before, this task alone can be intimidating. We present requirements interviewing techniques, concepts, and ideas in this book to help beginners figure out where to start, to help practitioners add to their bag of tricks, and to initiate a discussion amongst experts regarding the best practices for this evolving and challenging task.

Online resources for you:

⇨ View this chapter as a FREE video
http://businessanalysisexperts.com/lesson/what-is-requirements-elicitation/

⇨ FREE video: What Are Requirements?
http://businessanalysisexperts.com/product/what-are-business-requirements-stakeholder-solution/

⇨ Why Do Projects Fail?
Classic Mistakes by the International; Project Leadership Academy
http://calleam.com/WTPF/?page_id=799

⇨ Why Do Projects Fail?
US Census Bureau – Field Data Collection Automation (FDCA) – Case Study
http://calleam.com/WTPF/?p=1894

BEST PRACTICES FOR REQUIREMENTS INTERVIEWS

This chapter will help you:

- Plan, prepare, perform, and finalize effective requirements interviews

Proper Preparation Prevents Poor Performance

Planning and preparing requirements gathering interviews involves developing the right questions to ask, selecting the right people to answer the questions, and obviously managing the logistics of the interview. It means:

- ☑ having and expressing specific, measurable objectives for the interview

- ☑ knowing what questions you will ask the interviewee(s)

- ☑ preparing to capture the answers with minimal distractions (having a notepad or appropriate app for simple notes, diagrams, and/or recording the interview, etc.)

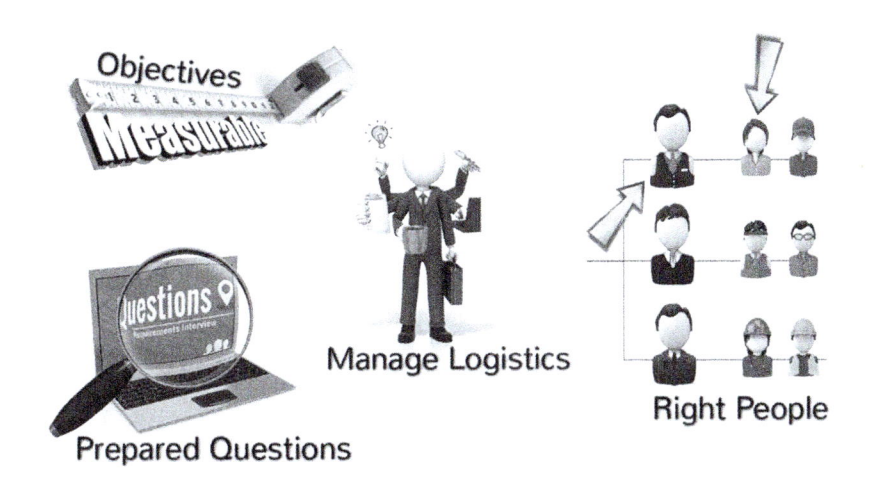

Prepared Questions **Manage Logistics** **Right People**

It also includes knowing and applying appropriate business analysis techniques to extract knowledge. For example, assume your objective is to define or clarify functional and non-functional requirements. Models or diagrams are great requirements discovery tools — but should you use swimlane diagrams, system flowcharts, data flow diagrams, or workflow models? Whichever modeling technique you choose, make sure you have the necessary software installed on a working computer before you start the interview.

As an alternative, do not forget to take a napkin to draw the diagrams on. You should also have a backup plan for the interview in case the technology does not work or the selected diagramming techniques do not deliver the results you need.

Being prepared also implies knowing as much as you possibly can about the person you are interviewing. For example, knowing the other person's stand on sensitive issues could make the requirements discovery interview much more productive.

Another dimension of being prepared is dressing appropriately for the interview. The old adage, "You never get a second chance to make a good first impression" is eternally true. If the requirements discovery interview is your first face-to-face contact, take the time to consider how you will dress. Back in the 1980s, there were great books like John T. Molloy's Dress for Success. It described exactly what type of suit to wear, what color of shirt with each suit, and which tie fit best depending on where you were doing business. Of course then the business world went business casual and threw our all of those recommendations – at least for the most part.

Our current recommendation for the one wearing the BA hat is to dress to put the interviewee(s) at ease. That again implies knowing something about them before you show up for the interview. If you are in doubt about your clothing, you might want to try Ann Marie Sabath's 2014 book, *Beyond Business Casual: What to Wear to Work If You Want to Get Ahead*.

Starting a Requirements Interview on the Right Foot

Performing the interview causes many wearing the Business Analyst hat to become anxious or nervous because it is where it all comes together. How can you make sure that your interview runs as smoothly as possible?

For starters, the first few seconds of any interview are critical.

We recommend starting the interview with small talk. Small talk puts people at ease and allows us to lower our guard. It helps everybody remember that we are all just people and that we are working toward a common goal.

The problem is there is only one safe topic for small talk and that is the weather. No one can do anything about it and everyone experiences it so that gives us the right to enjoy it, complain about it, and commiserate. Any other topic has the potential to backfire.

Assume that you happen to know that the person you are going to interview is a great football fan. You start the discussion by asking about a recent game. If his team lost, that could remind him about how upset he was with a ref's call and you might have just blown the interview.

Therefore, while we recommend small talk, you had better know the individual well enough to pick a safe topic or start with comments about the weather — or something equally disarming. If you do not know the individual, you might consider some type of icebreaker, like telling a good (safe) joke, revealing something funny about yourself, or something similar. There are tons of books available on effective icebreakers, just be very confident that whatever you try will not backfire.

A little experience goes a long way here because many people are nervous about being interviewed. They might be afraid of giving you wrong information and being held accountable later. If you are doing a group interview (a.k.a. Requirements Gathering Workshop), there is a much higher risk of this because other people are listening as well.

Whether you are conducting a 1-on-1 interview or a Requirements Gathering Workshop, take the time to put the interviewee(s) at ease. Give them an opportunity to express any expectations or concerns that they might have about the interview.

Ask them directly if you can do anything to help them contribute more fully. By the way, it is even important to listen to their small talk. Getting to know about people's lives helps you understand where they are coming from and that can help you tremendously in establishing the rapport you are going to need for the interview to run successfully.

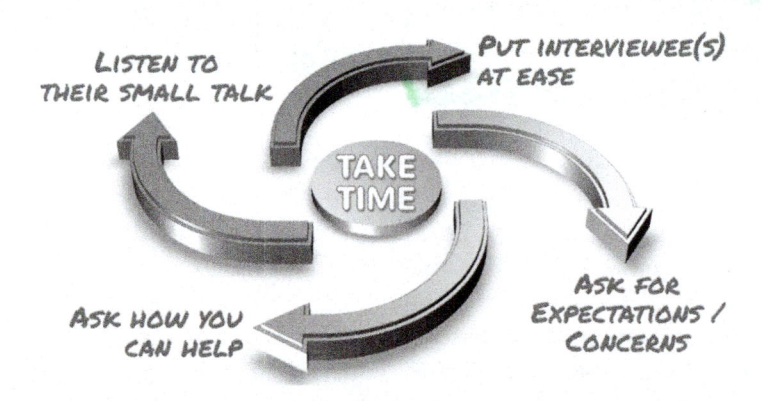

You can also put the interviewee(s) at ease up front by explaining **why** you need the information. Mention the project sponsor's title and name, state or restate the project objective, or reiterate the objective of this specific interview. Above all, make sure that the interviewee has an opportunity to ask any pertinent questions.

It is also important to create and maintain a safe climate. Make certain that the person you are interviewing does not feel threatened by your questions and feels that they can contribute freely with any answer. The better you are at putting them at their ease in the initial phases of the interview and keeping them at ease throughout, the more productive the entire requirements interview will be.

Performing under Pressure

Now that you have a great start, it is important to keep the momentum of the requirements interview going. One factor of maintaining momentum is nonverbal communication. As the one wearing the BA hat, you need to be able to recognize what signals people are sending with their nonverbal cues. You should also be conscious of what signals you are sending to them non-verbally!

At the simplest level, non-verbal communication is about recognizing how comfortable people are saying something, how confident they are in their answers, and how engaged they are in the topic. It is about assessing things like posture, comfort being close to each other, the sound of the voice, and the degree of culturally appropriate eye contact.

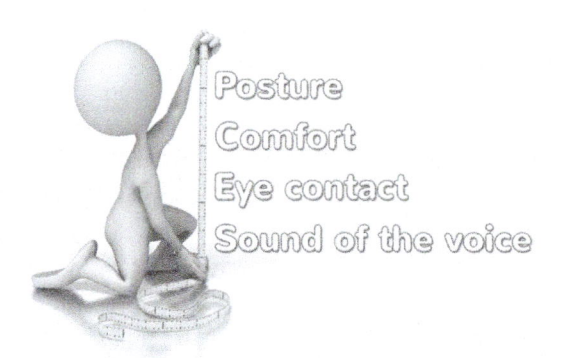

- Posture
- Comfort
- Eye contact
- Sound of the voice

Reading body language is a big part of non-verbal communication. Unfortunately, it is extremely complicated. As human beings, we acquire the ability to read body language while growing up. The culture and the people surrounding us influence how we read others. As we get to know people, we recognize their individual signs and personal idiosyncrasies that help us read their body language. It is much more difficult to read the body language of someone you do not know well, but there is a ton of research to get you started. Teaching you how to read body language far exceeds the scope of this presentation. Fortunately, a lot of that research on the topic is available on the Internet and studying it can drastically improve your interviewing skills. If you become proficient at reading body language and other non-verbal cues, you can extract more knowledge from what a person **does**

not say than from what he or she says – often even more than he or she would like you to know.

UNDERSTANDING BODY LANGUAGE

EASY   **MORE DIFFICULT**   **EVEN MORE DIFFICULT**

Another component of non-verbal communication is how a person speaks. When you ask an interviewee a question, listen carefully to the response. Pay attention to things like the timing and pace of the speech, how loud he or she speaks, the tone and inflection of the voice. Whether you are aware of it or not, your subconscious gets more information out of the sound of the voice than it gets out of the words.

That does not imply that what the interviewee says is unimportant – the words are the essence of the message. How they deliver the message, however, tells your subconscious whether the interviewee is honest and forthcoming, insecure, confident, being careful not to disclose something, and much more. Here again, research the web for tips on interpreting vocal cues.

Once the interviewee(s) finishes answering your question, verify what you understood by paraphrasing the answer. Paraphrasing is not repeating the words the interviewee said, but trying to express the intent behind the words. What was he or she really trying to communicate? The better you are at trying to paraphrase their intent, the more likely you are to identify potential misunderstandings.

Paraphrasing
EXPRESS THE INTENT!

IDENTIFIED MISUNDERSTANDINGS

Anytime you hear the interviewee say anything that implies an assumption, such as "I think", "I'm not sure", "I understand that …", and similar words, make a note of it and ask follow-on questions. I do not necessarily recommend taking the time to formulate a question immediately as this could interrupt the interviewing process. Just make sure that you do not forget to ask the clarifying question later and get the information and that you need.

If, at some point in time, the interviewee does not have an answer for one of your questions, let him or her know that it is fine if they do not know the answers to every question you are asking. This is important to keep them feeling comfortable and secure.

Avoid asking leading questions (e.g., "Have you quit beating your wife?" or "When did you stop cheating?"). They are provocative and put the interviewee on the defensive. They are phenomenally effective questions when used in an interrogation. However, they have no place in a requirements interview. Try to avoid even the hint that your interview is an interrogation.

Most often, you want to ask open-ended questions, meaning questions that will permit the individual to give you a lot of information in response. There are times however, when closed-ended questions are just as valuable. In particular, when you are trying to confirm information that the individual gave you, a closed-ended question might be appropriate.

For example, an open-ended question might be, "Give me an idea of the different types of transactions the application will have to process."

Once you get that information, you might follow up with a closed-ended question, "How many transactions do you anticipate the application to be processing every day?"

When she or he responds, "250 to 500", you might paraphrase the information by saying, "I understand then that we anticipate a minimum of 250 and a maximum of 500 of all types of transactions in any given 60-hour period. Is that correct?"

Make Sure You Can Talk the Talk

Every domain and every organization speaks its own language. Your interviewee(s) have their own domain language and may use terms unfamiliar to you. Even worse, they may use terms you think you understand but which have a very different meaning in their domain than in yours. If you would like to test this hypothesis, ask people in Sales, Finance, and IT for a definition of the term "Account". You will find three very different concepts.

ACCOUNT =

Finance — Sales — IT

In your interviews, always confirm that you and the interviewee both share a common understanding as to what a term means in the context of the interview. Miscommunication during a requirements interview is one of the biggest obstacles to developing effective requirements.

It is important that both you and the interviewee are comfortable with the interview, its pace, the progress you are making, and where you are going with the interview. If you start to feel uncomfortable, it is quite likely that the interviewee(s) will recognize it and feel equally uncomfortable. Quite often, the feeling of discomfort comes because your subconscious is trying to tell you that there is a potential for misunderstanding. Take time during the interview to identify and clarify any potential misunderstandings.

As a good interviewer, you want to stay focused on the topic that you scheduled the interview to cover. Nonetheless, do not neglect the human element. Allow some time for side remarks, jokes, and perhaps even a small diversion from the topic, but remember that you have to complete the interview and achieve your objective. You have to stay focused to complete your task within the allotted time.

A great way to maintain the focus is to post the questions somewhere that is visible to both you and the interviewee during the interview. Once you have a complete answer for a specific question, cross it off the list. This visible progress indicator lets you and the interviewee(s) see that you are making progress but that you still have work to do.

This technique is especially critical when you are having fun with the interview! If you and your subject matter experts are discussing something that is off topic but that is of interest to both of you, you are establishing rapport and that is great. However, be aware of time and possibly recommend carrying on a private conversation after the interview to chat about those things. For some people, it is all too easy to let the interesting and personal dimensions of life distract them to the point of neglecting to finish the interview and achieve its objective.

Maintain Control throughout the Requirements Interview

Conducting a successful interview requires that you maintain control. You are responsible for knowing where the interview is going at all times. Building rapport is one of the key components of maintaining control. Rapport is about a shared trust. The interviewees should feel confident that you know what you are doing. At the same time, you have to give them the feeling that you trust their domain expertise.

However, do not let the interviewees take over the interview and dictate the questions. That would put the interview at risk. Maintain rapport throughout the interview not by feigning interest but by being genuinely interested in what the interviewee has to say. The effort you put into planning and preparing the interview pays off in allowing you to maintain control of the interview.

Staying on topic is also an important part of conducting any successful interview. However, there may be times when you feel it is appropriate to deviate from the original topic of the interview for reasons that only become obvious during the interview. There is nothing wrong with that, as long as you maintain rapport with the interviewee so they know where you are going, why you are going there, and are willing to go with you. Conducting a successful interview is a collaborative effort between an interviewer and one or more interviewees.

A very simple approach for keeping the discussion on topic is to capture tasks that someone has to do after the interview. We call this your "Action Item" list. This list should not be visible to the interviewee(s) during the interview or it can distract more than it helps. Add items to the action item list as they come up but avoid lengthy discussions about them. Simply jot down 3 – 5 words that will remind you and the interviewee what someone has to do later. As soon as the item is noted, steer the discussion back to the topic at hand.

We also recommend the use of a separate "Question File" which lists the questions you want the interviewee to answer during the interview. If the interview uncovers additional questions that you need answered, add them to the question file and try to determine who is best qualified to answer the question. The combined use of the Question File and the Action Item list will contribute greatly to keeping the interview on track.

To reiterate, our keys for conducting a successful requirements interview are:

- ☑ Putting and keeping the interviewee at ease by creating and maintaining a safe climate

- ☑ Reading, capturing, and reacting to their non-verbal cues as well as to what they say

- ☑ Always clarifying assumptions, both theirs and yours

- ☑ Avoiding provocative, leading questions

- ☑ Speaking their language and ensuring that you share a common understanding of all terms

- ☑ Staying focused and in control throughout the interview

- ☑ Maintaining an Action Item list and review it at the end of the interview

Closing the Requirements Interview in Style

Regardless of which requirements interviewing approach you conduct,

1-ON-1 *TELECONFERENCE*

INFORMAL *EMAIL* *WORKSHOP*

do not forget to finish the interview in style. In closing the interview, ask something like, "Is there anything I didn't ask that you thought I should have?" or "Do you have any questions for me?" If there are no questions, recap the results either by giving the interviewee(s) an opportunity to read the notes you took or by reading the notes aloud.

If you had the luxury of having someone else taking notes from the interview, this is the only time in which he or she should speak. If the notes were not visible during the interview, ask the note-taker to read them aloud and present any models or diagrams.

Listening to what the note-taker jotted down and comparing it to your memory of the interview is a great way for spotting inconsistencies. You and/or the interviewee(s) can take exception, make corrections, add additional information, or do whatever is necessary to right any wrongs with the notes, models, or diagrams before the interview is finished.

Review the Action Items that you captured during the interview that either you or the interviewee(s) have do later. Do the same for unanswered questions, which are their own version of an action list. Revisit these items at the end of the interview and confirm that they are still necessary. If they are, assign each Action Item to one person present at the interview. That does not imply that the assigned person has to do the task necessarily; it simply means that the named individual is responsible for the task's completion. Anytime you assign a task, do not neglect to assign a due date on which it would be appropriate to remind the responsible party if the task is still open. In our experience, no interview has ever ended without an action list.

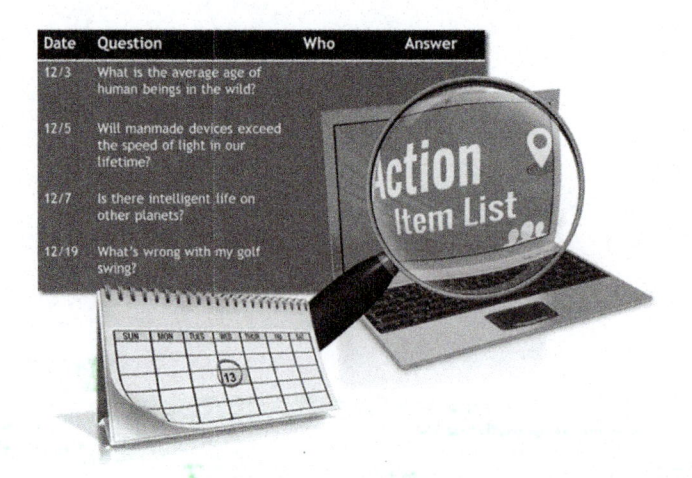

Finally, we also highly recommend thanking the interviewee(s) for their time and for the information provided. Ask them if they would be willing to give you a quick evaluation of the interview. On the next page, we give you an example of a 3-minute interview evaluation questionnaire that we have used for many years and that has helped us improve our interviewing techniques drastically.

Three-minute Interview Evaluation Form

On a scale of 1 – 5 (1 = excellent, 5 = sucks), how would you rate:

Topic	1	2	3	4	5
Your understanding of the objective of the interview in advance					
How well the interview met the stated objective					
The overall value of this interview to you					
The interviewer's interviewing (people) skills					
How confident are you that the information you provided was captured correctly					

What 3 things did you like least about this interview?

_____
_____
_____
_____

What 3 things did you like most about this interview?

_____
_____
_____
_____

We greatly appreciate the time you invested in giving us this feedback. Positive or negative, we will use it to improve the quality and outcome of future interviews.

Thank you for your participation and evaluation.

To paraphrase a famous quote,

> It ain't over when it's over

The first post-interview step that we recommend is reviewing your notes from the interview whether you did them yourself or you had a note-taker. Clean them up and, if appropriate, create a synopsis, put them in an email or any other acceptable mode of communication, and send that to the interviewee(s). This gives them a final chance to review what you heard. If the interviewee at this point comes back with a change to what you captured, that is not an indictment of your interviewing skills; it is an indication that you are successful in your follow-up.

Thank You!

Obviously, action items imply that action will happen. If you said anything during the interview that you would do, do it and let the interviewee(s) know you did it. If the interview called for an action item to clarify a point, send the clarification to the interviewees so that you can discuss any discrepancies. As a final note, we close almost every e-mail with a "Thank You" because we believe that is one of the most underused phrases in the English language.

Online resources for you:

- ⇨ What Questions Do I Ask During Requirements Elicitation?
  http://www.bridging-the-gap.com/what-questions-do-i-ask-during-requirements-elicitation/

- ⇨ How to Become More Confident in Requirements Elicitation
  http://www.bridging-the-gap.com/how-to-become-more-confident-in-requirements-elicitation-confidence/

- ⇨ CPMS | Requirements Gathering Interviews
  https://www.youtube.com/watch?v=R4vVooBM06Q

CHARACTERISTICS OF AN EFFECTIVE REQUIREMENTS INTERVIEWER

This chapter will help you:

- Describe and evaluate 9 practices that will improve the outcome of your requirements interviews
- Use active and informational listening techniques to get more information from your requirements interviews
- Recognize the impediments to these effective listening techniques and take steps to avoid them

Personable People Have a Head Start

Some people are just natural at interviewing other people; the rest of us could achieve similar results if we had a few tricks up our sleeves that would make the best use of our time and that of the interviewee(s). Chapter 5 presents attitudes and behaviors that people who are successful requirements interviewers exhibit. Analyze these characteristics and compare them to yourself to determine which work well for you and which you might want to work on to improve your interviewing skills.

Effective interviewers enjoy talking with other people regardless of their race, gender, political persuasion, religious beliefs, job title, or any other trait that you might use to categorize individuals. The best requirements discovery interviewers are engaging and if the interviewee enjoys talking with you, you are halfway home. Being personable is not about genetics, so you do not inherit it – you learn it. It is the ultimate social skill. It is about really listening and being genuinely interested in what the other individual thinks and says. It involves body language reinforcing your interest and empathizing with the interviewee. Above all, personable people make everyone around them feel good about themselves.

Avoid Biases and Prejudices

In the interview, a good interviewer avoids bias and prejudice. If the interviewer starts the requirements discovery interview with a personal bias for or against the interviewee or the topic, it will influence the questions and skew how the interviewer interprets the responses.

The interviewer should also avoid bias toward a specific solution, in particular during the early interviews. As the analysis progresses, you may start to lean toward one particular solution based on the requirements you gathered from other interviewees. For instance, you might be convinced that a sophisticated Cloud Storage solution would solve everyone's problems but the project sponsor might only be interested in sharing files via email. We recommend staying very open-minded about anything that comes your way during each interview and throughout the requirements discovery process.

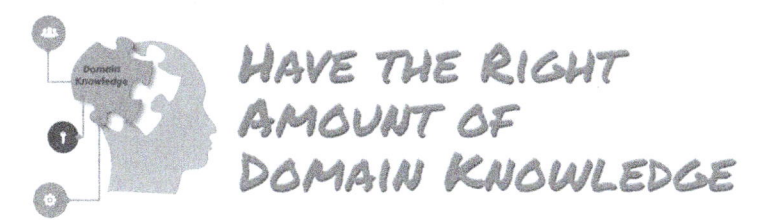

Have the Right Amount of Domain Knowledge

As the interviewer, you have to be knowledgeable about the topic of the interview. The key question is really, "How knowledgeable should you be?" meaning how much should you know about the topic to be effective. Fundamentally, the person conducting a requirements discovery interview should not know more about the topic than the subject matter expert they are interviewing. Otherwise, there is a high risk that the interview will end up being a lecture. That is particularly true if the interviewee(s) know that the interviewer is more knowledgeable than they are.

Having said that, the interviewer should understand the general business language and associated terminology of the interviewee. You should recognize idioms and terms germane to the topic, common abbreviations, and/or be an extremely quick study so you can learn the vocabulary, abbreviations, idioms, etc. during the requirements discovery interview. In addition, you can leverage your lack of knowledge by asking for a definition or explanation of terms with which you are unfamiliar. This approach actually keeps the interview moving and allows you to compare the definitions of individual interviewees to identify potential miscommunication and misunderstandings.

Maintaining Momentum during the Requirements Interview

PRACTICE GOOD Time Management

Effective interviewers practice good time management. Arrive a couple of minutes ahead of the scheduled time for the interview and quit a couple of minutes before the scheduled end. Those two behaviors send a significant signal to the interviewee that you value their time as well. If you are in the middle of a great interview and the allotted time is up, quit. If the interview really was as good as it felt, you should have discovered a ton of requirements that you need to analyze.

Once you take the time to consider all of this new-found knowledge, you will almost certainly have follow-up questions that allow you to drill down to lower levels of detail. Do not blow a perfectly good requirements discovery interview by overstaying your welcome. That sends the signal that you are not an effective time manager and can make it more difficult to schedule the next interview

STAY FOCUSED ON THE TOPIC

While discussing requirements with a stakeholder, stay focused on the topic at hand. Being focused helps you keep the discussion on track and makes it more likely that you will finish on time – or earlier. The danger of losing focus is that both you and the stakeholders can be sidetracked discussing a topic that is fascinating to both parties. Ask yourself if the topic is important to your project and contributes to achieving the objective of the interview, namely to discover requirements. The time you spend discussing inconsequential topics reduces the time you have available to cover the topics you really need to cover.

A good technique for staying focused on requirements discovery is to have a list of critical questions readily available, either in printed form or (even better) electronically. Whenever the interviewee starts going off on a tangent, you can always refer back to your list of questions. If the tangent intrigues you, suggest a different time to get together to discuss it in detail — maybe even after work, like over beer, wine, or cocktails.

Ask the Right People the Right Question

To make the requirements interview as effective as it can be, the interviewer asks the right people the right questions. Knowing what to ask the interviewee(s) is a critical success factor. Do not ask a senior manager questions about the work flow in their department or you could get an answer that is not up to date. Contrariwise, do not expect someone who works in the trenches to be capable of making strategic corporate decisions. Study the interviewee's job description before the interview to be able to decide what level of question is appropriate for the individual.

We also recommend giving the interviewee advance notice of what kind of information you are seeking in the requirements discovery interview. Sharing the specific questions gives the interviewee time to prepare and saves time in the interview. The time spent in getting to know and preparing the individual you are interviewing ahead of time can bring tremendous payoffs in terms of the quality of answers you get.

Using Active and Informational Listening to Hear Requirements

Getting requirements from others is a core competency for anyone wearing the BA hat, and conducting requirements gathering interviews is one of the primary techniques you need to do this well. The key question is how does one become good at interviewing other people? Whenever we ask that question in our instructor-led classes, the first answer we get is, "You have to be a good listener!". The question then becomes, "OK, what does that really mean? What makes someone a good listener?"

There are two specific listening techniques for ensuring that you are actually hearing what the other person is saying. The two techniques are **Active Listening and Informational Listening**.

Active Listening

Most people are familiar with the concept called *Active Listening*. Active Listening means sending signals so that the individual talking *recognizes* that you are listening. Simple ideas such as maintaining eye contact, nodding as the other person makes a point with which you agree, responding with verbal cues such as, "I understand", "OK", or "Yes" are all good Active Listening techniques.

Another key component in Active Listening is paraphrasing what the interviewees said when they have made a point. However, it is important to use different words than the original speaker did. Active Listening is a great tool for maintaining that essential rapport with the person you are interviewing.

If the interviewee gets the feeling that you are not actively listening because you are too busy taking notes, it can ruin an interview. That is the primary reason that we recommend splitting the roles of interviewer and note taker in requirements gathering interviews.

INFORMATIONAL LISTENING

Beyond Active Listening, there is a lesser-known concept called Informational Listening. That sounds intriguing, especially given the nature of the requirements gathering interview that you as the one wearing the BA hat are conducting. Informational Listening is really all about making sure that you are extracting the appropriate content and context from what people tell you.

As human beings, we often say many things that are relevant to the topic at hand. Unfortunately, we also say things that are not so relevant. Informational Listening is about utilizing the difference between these two situations to extract the essence of the discussion. You can imaging just how important this concept is in requirements gathering interviews.

For instance, if the person you are interviewing says, "Man, I have to tell you that we waste a ton of time correcting the initial premiums that the system recommends based on the incorrectly calculated age of the insured. It really gripes me that you people in IT cannot get that right! I do not know how many times we have told you to base the premium on the age the insured person will be six months from the effective date of the policy. Is that so hard to comprehend?"

The key informational component is the business rule:

> **BUSINESS RULE**
> Policy premiums are based on the age the insured party will be six months after the effective date of the policy.

The emotional outburst and the interviewee's justifications for the emotion distract many interviewers. It is easy to focus on feelings that the tirade evokes and miss capturing the business rule (which is the key informational component). One aspect of Informational Listening is to not criticize or analyze either the message or the messenger — just take it all in and file it for later use.

Impediments to Effective Listening

So what makes Active and Informational Listening so difficult? According to studies, three factors impede effective listening.

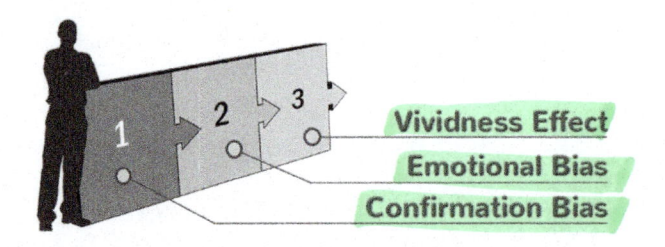

1. Vividness Effect
2. Emotional Bias
3. Confirmation Bias

Confirmation bias has to do with how the human brain works. When somebody makes a statement that confirms my belief, I get distracted feeling good about myself because we agree on an issue. While I am distracted, I might miss what the interviewee(s) says after that.

For example, assume that I am a football fan and I believe that the Tampa Bay Buccaneers could be a much better team if they had a better defensive line. Further, assume that the individual I am interviewing makes the statement "Tampa Bay would be so much better off if they just had a different offensive coach". I might zero in on the phrase "Tampa Bay would be so much better off" which confirms my belief but easily miss the fact that the other person is recommending a very different course of action than I would. That is confirmation bias.

A second hurdle that impedes Informational Listening is **emotional bias**. If you are in a heated discussion with an individual, you are less likely to be able to focus on the informational content of what he or she is saying. When people are angry, they are not listening to the provided information but are looking for a justification for their emotion. Emotional bias is something that you obviously have to avoid during the requirements gathering interview.

Unfortunately, sometimes the person you are interviewing will trigger your negative emotions and cause you to lose sight of what they are actually trying to tell you. Finding ways of coping with emotions is obviously beyond the scope of this book. It is important, however, to recognize that emotions play a major role in interfering with your ability to apply good Informational Listening.

The third impediment to Informational Listening is the **vividness effect**. This is something that happens in your brain whenever somebody mentions a topic that is associated with deep emotional ties or some event that had a very vivid impact on you. If you are the victim of a car crash, and somebody casually mentions a minor accident, the vividness effect can take over and cause you to start thinking about your personal experience instead of listening to what the other person is saying.

Another great example of the vividness effect is emotionally charged dates, such as September 11. Anytime anyone mentions that date or references "9-11", my thoughts immediately go back to where I was on that day and what I was doing. At that point, I am no longer really listening to what the individual is saying. I am experiencing the things that I went through on that day in my personal life. If you are a member of the older generation, December 7 (the attack on Pearl Harbor) and Nov 22 (the Kennedy assassination), are charged dates that could be equally detrimental to effective Informational Listening.

Overcoming the Impediments

The first step in dealing with these impediments to effective listening is to recognize them.

STEP 1
- Confirmation Bias
- Emotional Bias
- Vividness Effect

If you catch yourself experiencing the vividness effect, emotional bias, or confirmation bias, bring it up immediately with the person you are interviewing. Say something like, "I'm sorry, but I seem to have tuned out for a second. Could you repeat that, please?"

Oh! Sorry, but I seem to have tuned out for a second. Could you repeat that, please?

Acknowledging that it is happening limits the consequences of missing information that may be crucial to the goal of the requirements gathering interview.

Because this field is very new, we suggest doing additional research to learn more about Informational Listening. How can it improve your skills as an interviewer? Assuming that you are not interviewing the person to get a gauge of their feelings but to get information about their requirements for a proposed new IT solution, Informational Listening just might be the best technique you can find for achieving your goal.

Taking Advantage of Highway 350

Finally, there is a concept called Highway 350. Anyone who has taken one of our instructor-led classes has heard about this idea; whether they remember it or not is a different question. Studies have shown that most people can listen to another person talk at a rate of 500 words per minute and understand every single word the speaker is saying. The average speaker, on the other hand, speaks at a rate of 150 words per minute. The difference between the two is 350 (500 minus 150 — go ahead; you have a computer, check my math). That means that you have 350 words of listening capacity that the speaker is not utilizing.

We call it Highway 350 because it is down that road that your thoughts go zooming off toward the horizon, even while you are listening to every single word that the speaker says. This by itself is neither a good nor a bad thing. It just is. The critical question is, "How are you utilizing Highway 350?"

If you are using it to try to figure out how to dispute the interviewee's statements, what is for dinner, who is for dinner, or something like that, it becomes a major distractor and you might as well not be in the conversation at all. If, however, you use Highway 350 to apply the Active and Informational Listening techniques presented earlier, it becomes a very powerful tool in your listening arsenal.

Go ahead, give it a shot. You will be amazed at what you hear sometimes. It might even be important and improve your requirements gathering interviews.

Summary of the Traits

To recap, an effective requirements discovery interviewer:

- ☑ Stays focused on the topic
- ☑ Is well prepared, dresses appropriately, and has a realistic objective
- ☑ Understands the technical language of the interviewee
- ☑ Practices good time management
- ☑ Is open-minded and avoids bias towards people and solutions
- ☑ Asks the right people the right questions
- ☑ Is personable and puts the interviewee at ease
- ☑ Understands and applies good listening techniques

We are not suggesting that these are the only traits of a good interviewer. Other candidates that students often mention when brainstorming traits in our seminars include things like being articulate, maintaining eye contact, taking good notes, and many others. We selected these specific traits because they are the ones our students identify most often in our brainstorming exercise. In our real-life experience, these traits have also proven to be critical success factors for effective requirements gathering efforts.

Online resources for you:

- ⇨ How to use interviews to gather requirements
  http://reqtest.com/requirements-blog/how-to-use-interviews-to-gather-requirements/

- ⇨ Interviewing Tips for Software Requirements Gathering
  http://blog.nuvemconsulting.com/interviewing-tips-for-software-requirements-gathering

- ⇨ Use these interviewing techniques to gather project requirements
  http://www.techrepublic.com/blog/tech-decision-maker/use-these-interviewing-techniques-to-gather-project-requirements/

HELPING STAKEHOLDERS DISCOVER REQUIREMENTS

This chapter will help you:

- Name five specific approaches to working with Stakeholders to get their requirements
- Select the best fit for your situation based on the pros and cons of each approach

What Are the Five Elicitation Approaches and Which Is the Simplest for Starters

A lot of initial uncertainty on a project comes from not knowing how to approach stakeholders to get their requirements. Should you interview each stakeholder individually or in groups? Whom should you interview first? What can you do to guide stakeholders to give you the information you need to formulate the right requirements? This chapter provides a comparison of five common approaches for eliciting requirements from stakeholders on IT projects. It defines each method and suggests some strengths and challenges of using each for your consideration. This knowledge will guide you in deciding which approach is best suited for your project when you are the one wearing the BA hat.

Before we delve into the nitty-gritty details of the interviewing process, let us talk about different approaches that will help you discover requirements. Distinguishing characteristics that determine the approach include the number of interviewers, the number of interviewees, how much preparation is involved, and the technology used. We will present and compare:

☑ Informal Requirements Interviews

☑ Formal, Face-to-Face Requirements Interviews

☑ Requirements Elicitation via Email

☑ Teleconferencing to Discover Requirements

☑ Requirements Gathering Workshops

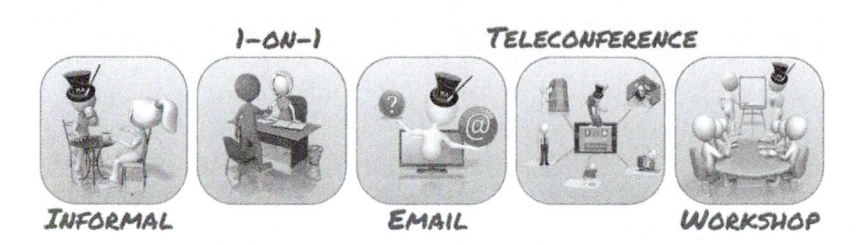

==The single unifying feature is that all of the above are interactions designed to get other people to discover, define, articulate, express, and potentially analyze their potential needs and requirements for a proposed IT solution.==

We will describe each approach, define the distinguishing attributes, and compare the relative strengths and challenges of each.

Informal Requirements Interviews

The first and simplest form is the accidental or informal interview. For example, you happen to run into an individual that you think might have some information you need. It can be in the hallway, over lunch, or even outside the workplace. The key about an informal interview is that it is unstructured and free flowing.

Although being informal, this type of interview requires that you are prepared. To take advantage of a situation requires that you know what information you need and who might have that information. Given modern technology, we recommend that you keep track of what you need on your smart phone, your tablet, or in any electronic device that you have with you at all times.

The Strengths of Informal Requirements Interviews

- 👍 Takes advantage of opportunities as they arise to discover requirements
- 👍 Interviewee is generally at ease because they are in natural settings
- 👍 Interviewee is more willing to share emotions and personal observations

The Challenges of Informal Requirements Interviews

- Interviewee has no time to prepare their answers
- Risk of the interviewee feeling ambushed
- Lack of structure can lead to sloppy thinking on both sides

Formal, Face-to-Face Requirements Interviews

Formal one-on-one interviews are planned, scheduled, and more-or-less structured interviews. They involve one or two subject matter experts (SMEs) and the one wearing the BA hat getting together in a face-to-face meeting to discuss the SME's problems and needs relevant to a proposed IT project. Use what you know you need to create an initial set of questions to start the interview. As this type of requirements interview progresses, the SMEs' answers will often trigger a host of follow-on questions that you may need to capture for other SMEs to answer.

Some ideas to consider for effective face-to-face interviews:

Location

We recommend scheduling this type of interview at the stakeholder's location. Quite often, they will need access to something that they use in their daily lives to give you the answer you need. In addition, most people feel comfortable and in control in their own workplace.

Taking Notes

Eye contact is a significant factor in human communication. If you are writing down what the interviewee is telling you, you are losing eye contact. That can be distracting. If at all feasible, we strongly recommend taking a colleague or peer to take notes, thus freeing you up to conduct the interview. If you follow this advice, however, make sure the interviewee knows there will be two of you. In addition, prepare for the interview by taking the time to discuss your note-taking strategy and expectations with your colleague. This ensures that both have a clear understanding of each other's role.

When you arrive for the interview, introduce the note-taker and clarify the roles for the interviewee. After introductions, note-takers should not speak until the end of the interview. If they speak, there is a high risk that the interview turns into an "inquisition" from the perspective of the interviewee. If they need clarification or misunderstand something the interviewee says, they can avoid interrupting the flow by jotting down a quick question for clarification at the end of the interview.

To put the final touch on your interview, allow the note-taker to read the notes aloud and pose those clarifying questions. This gives the note-taker an opportunity to clear up anything they did not capture. It also gives both the interviewer and the interviewee an opportunity to correct any misunderstandings. Having a designated note-taker allows the interviewer to focus on the interviewee and adds tremendously to the value of the interview.

Recording the Interview

If using a note-taker is not an option, another idea is to record the interview (assuming that the interviewee agrees). Given modern technology, you might consider using your smart-phone or tablet to record the interview (with or without a camera).

This ensures that you have access to the information and can analyze it at your leisure. Just remember that the stakeholder may not be as forthcoming with sensitive information (in particular when it involves human relationships) when they know they are being recorded (and as a side note, it is illegal in most jurisdictions to record them without their knowledge).

The Strengths of Formal Requirements Interviews:

- 👆 You and the interviewee have time to prepare yourselves for the interview

- 👆 Meeting face-to-face is generally non-threatening and the interviewer may be more willing to share personal thoughts and ideas

- 👆 It is easier to stay on topic and discover requirements when you are interacting with one or two people at a time

The Challenges

- Finding common time for an interview with SMEs can be a challenge; the knowledgeable people you need are usually the busiest

- If your project requires interviewing a large number of stakeholders, you may spend a lot of time reconciling the information you get from each with information you got from others

- It can be confusing to sort through the diverse answers you get from different stakeholders in individual one-on-one interviews to identify common threads

Requirements Elicitation Using Email

In today's world, it is increasingly rare to have the opportunity for a face-to-face meeting with the individual from whom you need information. Most organizations take advantage of modern technology and use email or some form of instant messaging for casual conversations. If you use these technologies for getting requirements, we call them silent interviews. They are quick, easy, and location independent.

Their ease of use should not detract from following some best practices to improve the reliability of the outcome. To ensure that the respondent gives you the answer you need, let her or him know why you need the information (e.g., "to ensure that the planned upgrade to the Inventory Management System meets your needs"). If you are using email, consider putting that in the subject line (most people scan the subject lines of their email to pick which one to open first; use it to grab their attention!)

Because it is an interview and you are trying to help them discover requirements, start with open-ended questions and use closed-ended questions to confirm details.

Open-ended question:	Close-ended question:
How does this work?	How many?

Keep your questions clear, short, and limited (in an IM exchange, only one question at a time; in an email, we suggest 5 – 9 numbered questions with sufficient space for the answer). To conclude an IM exchange or at the end of your email, always include a final open question like, "Anything I didn't think about that you would like to share?"

Schedule a date for the answer and if you do not get a response by that date, follow up. Depending on the corporate culture, you may have to consider what to do if you do not get a response even then. Time is the one universal resource we all have in equal amounts so do not forget to thank your interviewee for their time in advance. Once you receive a response, reply with follow-on questions to confirm or clarify their answers.

The Strengths of Interviewing via Email

- Instant documentation because the exchange is in electronic format)
- Location, time, and technology independent (you can even use your smart phone)
- The business community is very comfortable with these types of technologies

The Challenges

- The written word is easily misinterpreted
- Casual nature of the exchange can lead to answers that are not thought through
- Sensitive information may not be suitable for insecure electronic exchanges as there is a risk of exposure

Teleconferencing for Requirements

Most if not all of you probably have been involved in Teleconferences. To use a teleconference for getting requirements, you need to treat it like the group interview that it is. Prepare an agenda and a list of questions for the group. Share the list with all participants so the interviewees have time to prepare themselves. In addition, we strongly recommend using a teleconferencing tool with screen share capability. For sophisticated business analysis techniques such as process or data modeling, this feature is essential.

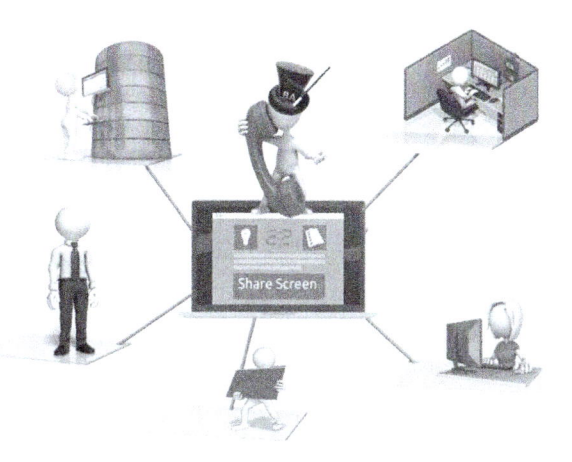

Whatever technology you use, you need a designated note-taker (not the interviewer) and/or plan to record the meeting. The latter of course mandates full disclosure to all participants and implies that you will spend a considerable amount of time after the teleconference analyzing the content. If the recording quality is not perfect, you may not be able to understand what was said. In addition, the interviewees may not be as willing to share sensitive information if they know you are recording their answers.

During the teleconference, you need to address every question to a named individual in the call. If you want to address multiple people with your question, you should ask it of each individual in turn starting with the highest-ranking person from whom you want an answer.

For many people, the biggest challenge with multi-person

teleconferencing is recognizing who is talking. Knowing from whom a requirement comes can be just as important as knowing what the requirement expresses. If the technology does not let everyone know who is speaking, we recommend requesting that every person preface their contributions with their name. All of the interviewing best practices that we present are just as important in a teleconference as in a face-to-face interview.

Best Practices

✓ **Informal Interview**
✓ **Formal Interview**
✓ **Email Interview**

Beyond that, there are many good sources online on how to run an online interview or facilitated meeting so we minimize that aspect of interviewing in this work.

The Strengths of Teleconferencing for Requirements

- 👍 Teleconferencing is cheap compared with travel costs required for face-to-face meetings (by the way, it is also healthier because there is much less probability of a contagious disease or cold spreading through the group if you are using teleconferencing)

- 👍 It is location-, time-, and technology- independent (you can even use your smart-phone or tablet)

- 👍 As opposed to email, you hear everyone's answer which gives you an additional sense for understanding what they really mean

The Challenges

- Unless the teleconference is extremely well moderated, people talk over each other and you may not be able to understand everything they say

- You have no knowledge or control over how focused the interviewees are on the topic. Many people multitask during teleconferences, which limits the value of their contributions.

- Although the vocal dimension adds information that allows you to evaluate the speaker's sincerity and confidence, you are still lacking the visual dimension with contains much more information

Requirements Gathering Workshops

Structured Group Interviews or Workshops are planned, scheduled, and formal working sessions. They have been around for a while under a variety of names and, of course, associated acronyms. You might be familiar with JAD (Joint Application Development), JRP (Joint Requirements Planning), JAR (Joint Application Requirements), or any number of similar concepts. For political reasons, the term Joint has pretty much fallen out of favor in recent years, so we as an industry are moving to the more neutral-sounding name "Requirements Gathering Workshops".

The primary goal of any Requirements Gathering Workshop is to define the features, functions, and requirements for a business solution typically including an IT (Information Technology) component. Since IT applications affect many diverse groups of people within an organization, these workshops give all stakeholders an opportunity to express their individual needs and desires. The main purpose of a Requirements Gathering Workshop is to shorten the time needed to create and achieve consensus within a cross-functional group on a complete set of non-redundant, prioritized, and valid requirements that define all aspects of the proposed business solution.

Due to the relative complexity of planning and conducting effective Requirements Gathering Workshops, we will delve into techniques later. To help you determine if a Requirements Gathering Workshop is the appropriate choice for your project, however, consider its relative strengths and challenges:

The Strengths of Requirements Gathering Workshops

- Leverages group dynamics allowing issues to be addressed immediately because all of the people involved hear what the other people have to say

- Generates a tremendous quantity of high-quality requirements in a very compressed time frame

- Builds a team ownership of the outcome and all attendees share a common understanding of the requirements

The Challenges

- Getting all necessary stakeholders to commit to a multi-day workshop can be next to impossible in today's multi-tasking business environment

- The results of the workshop have to be sold to those who could not attend

- Because of scheduling conflicts with critical people, this approach only works on mission-critical projects which have the highest priority in the organization. (Trust me, we have tried to use this technique on lower-priority projects; it has consistently delivered less than stellar results.)

As you can tell by now, each approach we presented has significant advantages and disadvantages. We realize that the listed strengths and challenges are incomplete but we hope they help you decide which approach is the best fit for your situation.

As the one wearing the BA hat, your responsibility is to pick the interviewing approach based on the people you need to interview and the information you need from them. Regardless of which approach you take, one final word of advice: do not involve people who have nothing to contribute to the topic. Idle spectators distract the interviewee and the interviewer, so make sure that everyone invited to your interview belongs there.

Online resources for you:

⇨ KnowledgeKnugget™ video: How to Identify Stakeholders for IT Projects
   http://businessanalysisexperts.com/product/what-are-business-requirements-stakeholder-solution/

⇨ Requirements Gathering Workshops for Widely Distributed Teams
   http://businessanalysisexperts.com/requirements-gathering-workshops/

⇨ Instructor-led class: How to Facilitate Requirements Gathering Workshops
   http://businessanalysisexperts.com/product/how-to-facilitate-requirements-gathering-workshops/

⇨ Methods for Eliciting - Not Gathering – Requirements
   http://www.batimes.com/articles/methods-for-eliciting-not-gathering-requirements.html

HOW TO RUN A REQUIREMENTS GATHERING WORKSHOP

This chapter will help you:

- Plan, prepare, perform, polish, and publish the outcomes of a Requirements Gathering Workshop

- Defend the need for each stage

How Requirements Gathering Workshops Work

Requirements Gathering Workshops are a special challenge for the one wearing the business analysis hat. The good news is that working with a cross-functional group of stakeholders to get their requirements is a fascinating and exhilarating experience when it works well. In this chapter, you will learn specific steps and recommendations for planning, preparing, performing, polishing, and publishing the results of effective requirements workshops to improve the odds that they deliver the results you need.

In the 1970's, a new concept called JAD (Joint Application Design) sessions emerged to address the challenge of delivering usable technology to the business community. The concept involved a weeklong workshop attended by the project sponsor, representatives from all affected business areas (including the IT development group), and a workshop facilitation team consisting of a facilitator and a documentation expert. The one-week pilot project designed a system that supported a hospital emergency room and enabled the developers to deliver the system in under a month versus the 18 months that was the accepted standard of the day.

The resounding success of that original JAD session generated immense enthusiasm for the concept. Whereas the pilot project actually defined and designed the entire application, it soon became apparent that it was not possible to get to that level of detail on all projects. As a result, current adaptations of the JAD concept (under a wide variety of acronyms) tend to focus more on defining the complete business solution as opposed to designing the technology.

In a nutshell, Requirements Gathering Workshops are time-compressed, cross-functional meetings that can span days. The goal is to get a complete set of non-redundant, prioritized business and stakeholder requirements that reflect the needs of all attendees.

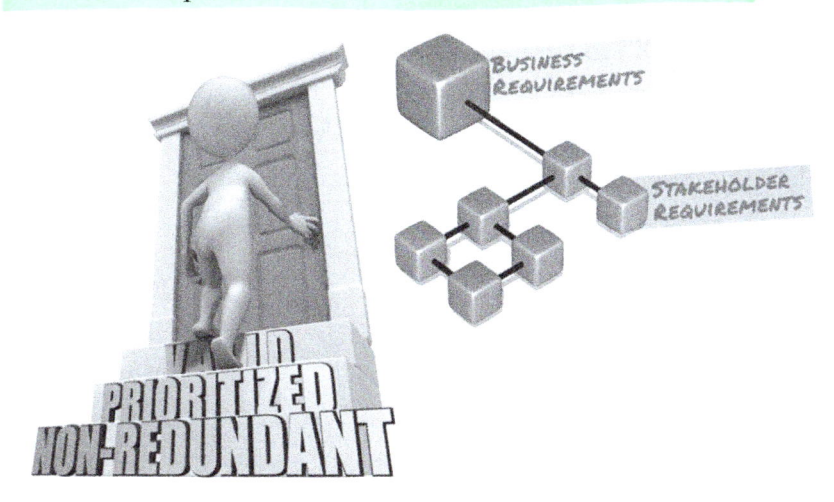

Getting good requirements from a group of stakeholders with different areas of responsibilities is a non-trivial activity. The

Requirements Gathering Workshop often involves concrete steps such as:

- ⇨ developing and presenting the business case
- ⇨ defining and analyzing business problems and potential solutions
- ⇨ drawing and using business process diagrams
- ⇨ creating and analyzing business information models
- ⇨ formulating business, stakeholder, and solution requirements

The specific activities of any Requirements Gathering Workshop differ. A well-structured and facilitated Requirements Gathering Workshop coordinates all selected activities to produce high quality, well founded, and agreed-upon requirements expressed in a format that IT developers, testers, and others responsible for developing the solution can understand and use.

To ensure a successful outcome, there are five segments to every Requirements Gathering Workshop, namely Planning, Preparing, Performing, Polishing, and Publishing. Each segment is critical to the ultimate success of the workshop.

Planning and Preparing for a Productive Requirements Gathering Workshop

1) Planning

The Planning segment generally lasts between 2 to 8 hours, depending on circumstances. The purpose of this segment is to:

- ⇨ determine whether a Requirements Gathering Workshop is the appropriate approach for this particular project,

- ⇨ determine the specific deliverables that a workshop will create

- ⇨ create a preliminary agenda for the Requirements Gathering Workshop if one is approved

- ⇨ pick the best available participants to attend

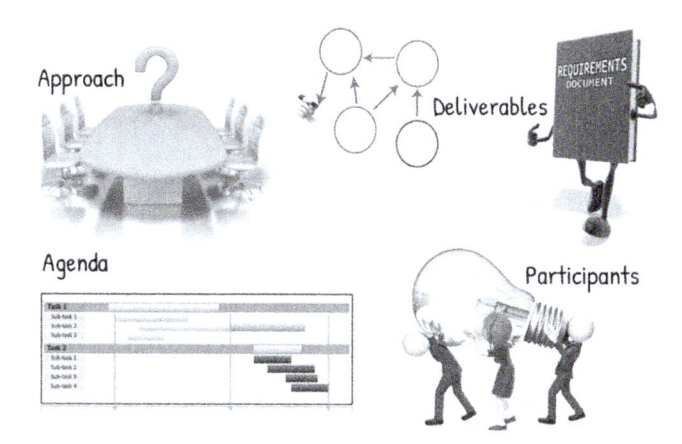

Approach

Deliverables

Agenda

Participants

The attendees for the Planning meeting include:

- ☑ the facilitation team who would run an approved Requirements Gathering Workshop

- ☑ the Project Sponsor

- ☑ the Project Manager/Leader

- ☑ the Lead Business Analyst(s) assigned to the project

- ☑ Managers of each functional area the project might affect

- ☑ Subject Matter Experts (SMEs) representing each functional area

- ☑ Someone with the authority to authorize a Requirements Gathering Workshop

② Preparing

As its name suggests, the Prepare segment gives those participants invited to attend the Requirements Gathering Workshop time to prepare themselves. The facilitation team uses this time to:

- select the appropriate techniques for each deliverable the workshop will produce

- flush out the preliminary agenda

- prepare any applications and templates needed for the session based on the selected deliverables

- make any necessary travel arrangements

- book facilities for the workshop

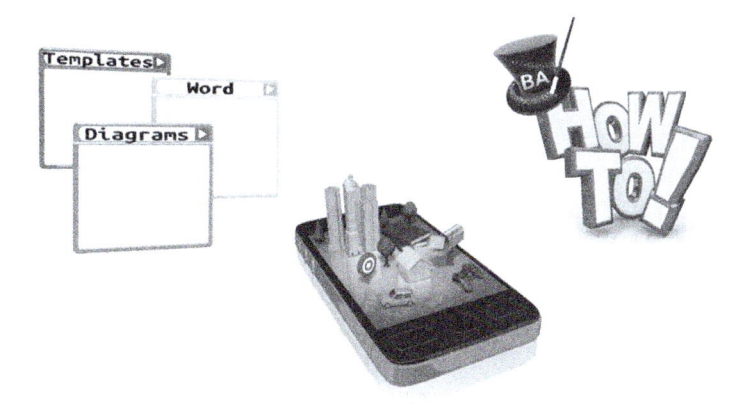

Invited Business Analysts and SMEs need this time to:

- ☑ discuss the project with their peers
- ☑ collect pertinent information for the workshop
- ☑ most importantly, get everything else off their plate for the duration of the Requirements Gathering Workshop

The Subject Matter Experts will participate full-time in the workshop for however long the workshop should last. As a result, they may need to find someone to take on some of their day-to-day responsibilities so they can be productive in the workshop.

How to Perform During the Workshop

3) Performing

The Perform segment is where the rubber meets the road (or something like that). A facilitation team consisting of a workshop Facilitator and an in-session business analyst (In-Session BA) run the workshop. The Facilitator is the public face in the front of the room. This individual guides the group through the process, teaches any techniques participants may not know, for example process modeling, problem analysis, requirements prioritization, etc. The Facilitator helps the group perform the techniques to flush out requirements. He or she also reacts to events by modifying the approach and potentially the agenda as appropriate. She or he is primarily responsible for the people side of the workshop.

The In-Session BA does the real work in a Requirements Gathering Workshop. Seriously, everyone involved does real work. Nonetheless, the In-Session BA has the thankless job of translating the essence of flowing group discussions into well-formulated requirement statements, user stories, or in the form of an appropriate diagram (e.g. use case models, process maps, data models, etc.) while conducting instant and on-going business analysis to ensure the quality of the work.

This individual sits in the session wired to a computer with an LCD projector and often works through breaks to maintain the momentum of the workshop. The on-screen visibility of information enables the group to rapidly identify discrepancies, resolve differences, and reach consensus.

The In-Session BA role is difficult to fill because it requires someone who is extremely confident in their use of business analysis tools and techniques and can react instantly to any change of course that the Facilitator decides is necessary to achieve the goal of the workshop. We personally know a lot more good Facilitators than we know good In-Session BAs. Both roles require exceptional business analysis skills, but very few business analysts are willing to play their trade under public scrutiny given the added element of intense time pressure.

Because of this challenge, some facilitation teams assign the Session Analyst a separate room. In that type of workshop, the Facilitator takes notes on a flip-chart or white-board and hands these off to the Session Analyst who transcribes them while the workshop group is working on the next deliverable. This approach requires a follow-on review of the deliverable by the workshop participants to clarify any discrepancies and/or misunderstandings.

Contributors are the real people in the room. They are the SMEs who have the knowledge and the authority to make decisions and technical experts who have questions and need answers to know what they should deliver to satisfy the needs of the business experts.

The makeup of these two groups is crucial for the success of the Requirements Workshop. You need the right business experts from all of the various functional areas that the solution will affect to give their input and blessings. You need informed, open-minded technical experts who are willing to listen to what the business community needs before suggesting a solution. The core rationale behind the elicitation concept is to gather as many requirements as possible from all involved stakeholders before making design and implementation decisions.

Advisors are non-participants with specific knowledge that the workshop participants need to complete a specific assignment. Advisors need to be available to support the workshop on very short notice, typically next business day at the latest. The Facilitator will notify the Advisors of the topic for which their guidance is required by submitting questions the workshop participants develop. They schedule a specific time slot (typically 1/2 – 1 hour) that fits the group's and the Advisors' schedules.

When the Advisor joins the workshop, Contributors ask the Advisors the prepared questions related to their area of expertise and the In-Session BA integrates the responses into the appropriate deliverable of the workshop. Obviously, the Contributors may also ask follow-on questions to clarify the answers. Advisors are not full-time participants in the workshop; they have to be available when needed and leave when they finish their contributions.

A Requirements Gathering Workshop produces three primary results:

- ☑ Preliminary versions of the deliverables (requirements, user stories, models, etc.) as identified during the workshop Planning phase

- ☑ A list of open questions, issues, and action items that need resolution to finalize the deliverables, and

- ☑ A much deeper understanding of what the project is really all about

Polishing and Publishing the Workshop Results

④ Polishing

The primary purpose of the Polishing segment is to find answers to the open questions, resolve the open issues, complete the action items, and finalize the preliminary deliverables from the workshop. In reality, most organizations also use the increased understanding of the project gained from the workshop to evaluate whether or not the project is really such a good idea after all. Now that they know a whole lot more, they have a better sense of just how big the project really is. This is an excellent time to revisit the project charter, goals, objectives, original estimates, and budget based on the new knowledge to see what they can do to increase the probability of a successful completion of the project. That includes, by the way if it is appropriate, cancelling it!

5) Publishing

The Publishing segment is a final wrap-up meeting. Ideally, the same people who attended the workshop would be present. The primary purpose of the meeting is to give everyone who was there an opportunity to report the status of the action items, finalize the drafts of the deliverables, and draw on the momentum generated by the Requirements Gathering Workshop to keep the project moving or to cancel the project if that is the right course of action. Without this wrap-up meeting, you have no real opportunity for a lessons-learned evaluation that does more to help future projects than any other single step you might take.

The Business Case for Requirements Workshops

According to past clients, facilitated Requirements Gathering Workshops reduce the time required for the initial requirements definition, elaboration, and analysis activities by up to 70%. Our clients based the estimated reduction on how long it had taken them historically to accomplish similar results on comparative projects without using a Requirements Gathering Workshop. We have facilitated Requirements Gathering Workshops for IT projects that used a Waterfall methodology and others that used Agile development approaches. The primary difference in the outcomes was the name and types of deliverables and the depth of detail that the individual Requirements Gathering Workshop delivered.

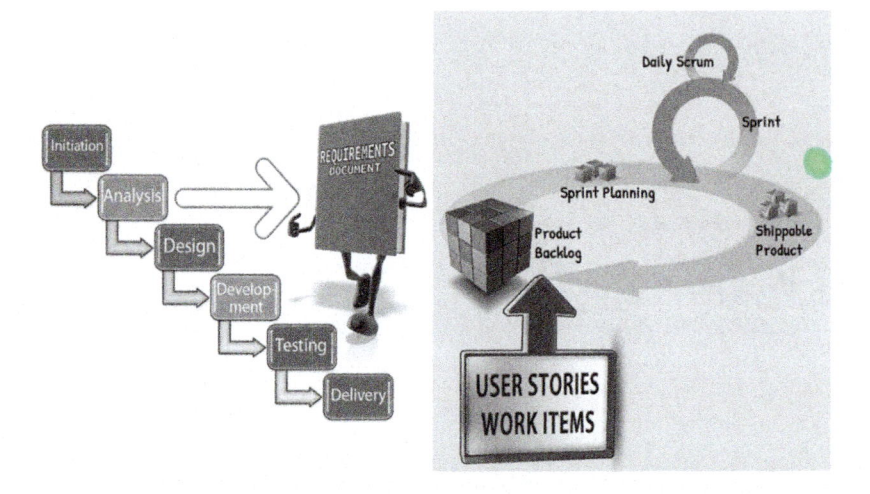

⇨ For Agile projects, user stories and work items created an initial product backlog

⇨ Requirements Gathering Workshops for projects following traditional approaches delivered Business and Stakeholder Requirements, Business Process Models, and Business Data Models that formed the core of a Requirements Definition Document (RDD)

A Requirements Gathering Workshop can span 2-3 days or be spread out over 4-6 weeks and can be virtual, face-to-face, or (ideally) a blend of both. A small group of peers attends virtual sessions to create initial results. A final, face-to-face, offsite session allows representatives from all groups to discuss and finalize the requirements while minimizing work-related interruptions.

To ensure that your project is a good candidate for a Requirements Gathering Workshop, consider the critical success factors:

- ☑ You need clear, public, executive support for your project
- ☑ Your project has to be the highest priority for the participants
- ☑ The contributors who will attend have to have the necessary expertise and authority
- ☑ The facilitation team needs to know all necessary business analysis tools and techniques intimately
- ☑ The facilities support the creative process, both virtual and/or live
- ☑ The deliverables have to be clearly defined, achievable, relevant, and time-bound
- ☑ You have to have appropriate automated tools to support the creation of the deliverables during the session

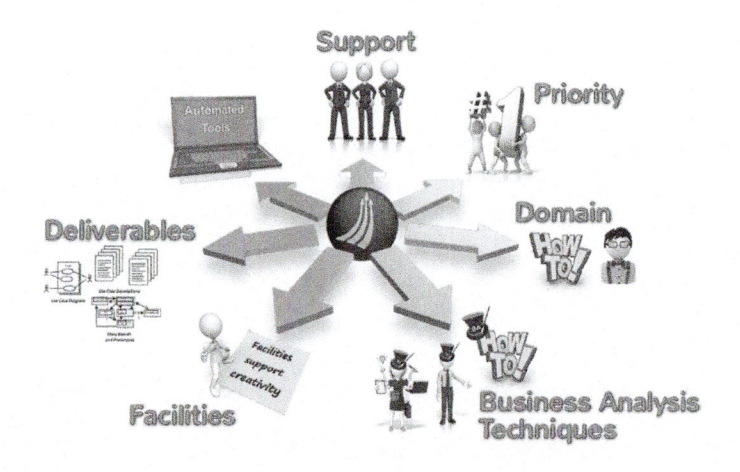

If your project meets these criteria, a Requirements Gathering Workshop can help you get the right requirements faster, cheaper, and better than conventional business analysis activities. If getting the right requirements rapidly is important to you, a Requirements Gathering Workshop delivers.

Online resources for you:

- ⇨ JAD Guidelines
  http://www.ksinc.com/itpmcptools/JADGuidelines.pdf

- ⇨ Methods for Eliciting - Not Gathering - Requirements
  http://www.batimes.com/articles/methods-for-eliciting-not-gathering-requirements.html

- ⇨ Using JAD for an Iterative Approach to Requirements Management
  http://www.batimes.com/articles/using-jad-for-an-iterative-approach-to-requirements-management.html

- ⇨ Six Common Problems Faced by a Business Analyst
  http://www.batimes.com/articles/six-common-problems-faced-by-a-business-analyst.html

REQUIREMENTS INTERVIEWS AND WORKSHOPS WRAP-UP

This chapter will help you:

- Review the contents of the book

- Prepare a plan for implementing new concepts

What Do You Do Next?

Conducting requirements discovery interviews and workshops is challenging and being a good interviewer is not easy. We encourage the one wearing the BA hat to be aware of the awesome responsibility she or he carries and recommend working on improving your interviewing skills continuously. As practicing business analysts ourselves, we practice what we preach. We believe that regardless how good you are, there is always room for improvement.

You now have several techniques and behaviors that will help you to plan, prepare, and execute requirements elicitation for IT projects. Actually, we maintain that many of the techniques we presented apply to any type of serious discussion, but in the context of this publication, we are only concerned with requirements elicitation for IT projects.

We cannot pretend that this publication covers every possible requirements elicitation technique. A thundering herd of other techniques exists for getting the business community to contemplate and express what they need a future IT solution to deliver. In this book, we have focused purely on collaborative techniques involving natural language. You can also use techniques like data flow diagrams, swimlane diagrams, data models, use case diagrams, and a slew of other modeling techniques to help the business community identify its needs. Visual representation of workflow and data dependencies can stimulate thoughts that go far beyond simple language. Keep expanding your repertoire of requirement gathering techniques.

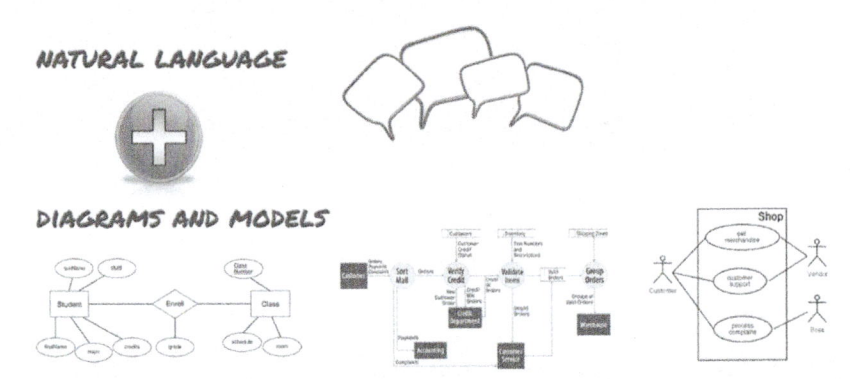

NATURAL LANGUAGE

DIAGRAMS AND MODELS

As your list of potential requirements grows, you might be rightfully concerned that you have identified far more requirements than your project can satisfy. In our opinion, that is not a problem but a bonus. Our goal is to minimize missing requirements and reduce scope creep caused by requirements identified late in the project. Consciously removing requirements that you cannot satisfy is considerably easier than seeing requirements that are not on the list.

If you are the one wearing the BA hat, you still have a lot of work ahead of you before you are done. Once you have the results of requirements elicitation, the next step is typically to formulate a complete, non-redundant, prioritized set of business and stakeholder requirements defining an acceptable solution. If you are working in an Agile environment, you might express the requirements as User Stories, Use Cases, or Work Items.

Those activities exceed the scope of this publication, but we do offer guidance on each of those topics in other publications and in our training curriculum.

In closing, we recommend against trying to implement every idea in the book at once. Pick 2 - 3 techniques or ideas for starters. Try them out in a real project and analyze the outcome.

If the techniques worked as-is, great. If any of our techniques do not work, you might want to review that section of the publication to see if you missed anything. If you think you are doing everything right and the technique still did not deliver the desired outcome, feel free to change it, adapt it, and make it work for you. Contact us at help@ba-experts.com if you have any questions or need additional guidance. Learning is about changing your behavior to acquire new abilities and adapting new techniques to your view of the world.

In addition, we appreciate any feedback you have on your experience. Shared knowledge increases exponentially, and we will continue to share our insights or epiphanies regarding how to best get the right requirements from the right people at the right time to make your IT projects succeed.

Do not forget, missing and misunderstood requirements are still the Number one cause of IT project failure and have been since we invented these things called computers. Anything you can do to reduce the risk of that happening to your projects will greatly enhance the probability of your personal and professional success.

ABOUT THE AUTHORS

Angela and Tom Hathaway have authored and delivered hundreds of training courses and publications for business analysts around the world. They have facilitated hundreds of requirements discovery sessions for information technology projects under a variety of acronyms (JAD, ASAP, JADr, JRP, etc.). Based on their personal journey and experiences reported by their students, they recognized how much anyone can benefit from improving their requirements elicitation skills.

Angela's and Tom's mission is to allow anyone, anywhere access to simple, easy-to-learn business analysis techniques by sharing their experience and expertise in their business analysis training seminars, blogs, books, and public presentations.

At BA-EXPERTS (http://businessanalysisexperts.com/) we focus exclusively on Business Analysis for **"anyone wearing the BA hat™"**. We believe that business analysis has become a needed skill for every business professional whether or not they have the title Business Analyst. We have made it our goal to enable anyone wearing the BA hat™ to have access to high quality training material and performance support. Please call us at 702-637-4573, email us (Tom.Hathaway@ba-experts.com), or visit our Business Analyst Learning Store at (http://businessanalysisexperts.com/business-analysis-training-store/) if you are interested in other training offers. Amongst other offers, the content of this book is also available as an eCourse on our website.

Printed in Great Britain
by Amazon